John O'Reilly is a performing arts presenter whose credits include producing:

1. *The Bolshoi Ballet*
2. *The Mariinsky Theatre (Kirov) Ballet*
3. *The Mikhailovksy Theatre Ballet.*

John was the executive director of the special care facility, Recovery Acres Society. He is now the president and owner of Harlequin Homes.

This book is dedicated to my daughter, Christine, and my son, Colin.

Grandchildren: Dashiel, Terriann, Byron.

Great-Grandchildren: Levi, Leonardo, Charlie, Jaxon, Mason, Colton, Emerson, Mary Jane.

Brothers and Sisters: Ann, Faye, Michael, Brent, Gary.

John O'Reilly

My Observations II

A small book of seeds and
meditation items

AUSTIN MACAULEY PUBLISHERS®

LONDON * CAMBRIDGE * NEW YORK * SHARJAH

Ordering Information
Quantity sales: Special discounts are available on quantity purchases by corporations, associations, and others. For details, contact the publisher at the address below.

Publisher's Cataloging-in-Publication data
O'Reilly, John
My Observations II

ISBN 9798889101987 (Paperback)
ISBN 9798889101994 (ePub e-book)

Library of Congress Control Number: 2023922544

www.austinmacauley.com/us

First Published 2024
Austin Macauley Publishers LLC
40 Wall Street, 33rd Floor, Suite 3302
New York, NY 10005USA

mail-usa@austinmacauley.com
+1 (646) 5125767

These observations are meant to be contemplated, pondered, and meditated upon one at a time. The book is meant to be very simplistic i.e. no direction or outcome expectations.

The Dance Teacher

It doesn't matter if, "when you grow up", you won't be a dancer. If you have to do one thing, dance done well doesn't just teach you how to dance or have a toned body. It teaches you harmonious and elegant movement.

Dance done well teaches much more. It teaches you to respect your working group, how to struggle to achieve a goal, that no one gives you anything, and to recognize the skill of your competitor in the event of defeat.

Dance teaches you to commit, organize, be responsible, and be honest.

These qualities, even if you are not a dancer, will be useful to you throughout your life. Whether you become a parent, a doctor, a lawyer, or an architect, during your growth journey, especially in an era that wants everything right away.

If you've learned to manage your time with responsibility and commitment, you'll definitely be a privileged person.

Notes

"The root of the problem is selfishness and self-centeredness."

Notes

"Don't die with the song still in you."

Notes

"Our business is improving life."

Notes

"When learning to hunt, follow the shark, not the dolphin."

Notes

"Shut up and listen."

Notes

"In order to be interesting, you must be interested."

Notes

"I've never seen a wild thing feel sorry for itself."

Notes

"When at the end of your rope, let go."

Notes

"The citizen is the highest member of society."

Notes

"One pair of baby shoes for sale, never worn."

Notes

"Trust yourself."

Notes

"If I am dealt a lemon, make lemonade."

Notes

"Sometimes the pot is too small for the plant to grow and needs replanting into a bigger environment."

Notes

"Keep working; it keeps the old person out."

Notes

"Many people live in the comfort of
their opinion without knowing the discomfort of thought."

Notes

"The growing up home was a house of 'no', but at grandma's house, it was a home of 'yes'."

Notes

"If someone is ignoring you, never disturb
that person again."

Notes

"Importance of story."

Notes

"Good judgment comes from experience, and experience comes from bad judgment."

Notes

"The best thing you can give an artist is a seed and a blank palette."

Notes

"Fail big."

Notes

"Give a compliment."

Notes

"Contribute and belong."

Notes

"Commit and have conviction."

Notes

"Titles are important: housewife, mother, wife, husband."

Notes

"If you are looking for a place, there is plenty of room at the top."

Notes

"I am blind; it's a beautiful day, and I can't see it."

Notes

"Dreams do take some effort."

Notes

"Don't tell me your faults, let me find
them on my own."

Notes

"Romancing the thought."

Notes

"We were created to create."

Notes

"Ask God to make a way where there is no way."

Notes

"Make God's heart sing, show out your gift."

Notes

"When I face adversity, I overcome fear."

Notes

"God does not give you anything you can't handle."

Notes

"Let it go; if it comes back, it's yours."

Notes

"Truth is precious."

Notes

"At the end of the day, this biker friend of mine, Josh, tells me to just say thanks, and if someone is listening, great, and if not, you haven't wasted too much time."

Notes

"Follow your dreams; if you don't, someone will hire you to follow theirs."

Notes

"Pray bold."

Notes

The theatre allows us to share in a connection like no other live performances, lets us examine who we are, where we have come from, and who we aspire to be. That aspiration for a better tomorrow motivates me.

Notes

My key to dispersing my anger is with a pen and paper. My anger was always just under the surface and developed over time, probably starting when I was a child living with a father who would come home drunk and terrorize the family. I started to learn how to journal when I stopped smoking, I wanted to replace the smoking habit with a new one. It was suggested to me to write down the good things that happened to me as a result of not having that cigarette. So every time the urge to smoke arose, I would write instead. At first, I could only get one or two sentences down, but after three months and filling several books, I could easily fill a whole page or two. It's been several years now, and I have never told myself or anyone else that I quit; I simply remind myself that I'm not having one right now. And even when the urge is strong, I tell myself that if I still feel this way tomorrow, I will smoke five packs, thankfully, I always felt better the next day. But back to the anger disbursement, I also learned a bit about journaling from that exercise. After an angry outburst triggered by a request from my favorite girlfriend, I knew I had to examine my anger. Acting out was becoming more my method of handling problems and was becoming part of my identity. So, with my new journaling skills, I decided to write out the biggest resentments that were bothering me. It wasn't very pretty at first, but I was able to get a few things down about my father, girlfriends, and some money transactions. Once I got my issues down and, what actually happened, which was very difficult at the start, I decided to write down how I responded and how I handled my part.

Asked myself what I would have liked to have done in that moment, I then expressed some pretty dark and violent thoughts that were on a piece of paper not acted out on. I finished up by saying a little prayer for everyone. I noticed that after a few days of doing that little exercise, those items didn't seem to have the same importance anymore. So I started using that little formula for every item in my life, starting from my first memory to the present. I spent three or four months writing something every day, and slowly, the anger started to disburse. As I was going through this exercise, a few surprises showed up, the big one was the patterns in how I handled things. It provided me with significant insights into myself. One of the hurdles I had to overcome was my identity. The anger was part of my identity, serving as my protection and influencing my social skills and habits. I realized I had a lot of work to do in this area. I also found out that the root of the problem was selfishness and self-centeredness. It's taken a while to come to terms with a lot of things, but it's been a really exciting journey.

Notes

Additionally, Matt N. said to me, "You got this gift, what are you doing with it?"

Notes

"Our business is improving the quality of life."

Notes

IKIGAI

IKIGAI is a Japanese concept that means "Your reason for being." "IKI" means life, and "GAI" describes value or worth. Your IKIGAI is your life purpose or your bliss. It's what brings joy and inspires you to get out of bed every day.

I would like to acknowledge the following people for their inspiration:

Melissa Zuccala
J. Kennedy
B. Streisand
John Rook, PhD
Josh McEwen
M. O'Reilly